Air Fryer Recipes for Beginners

Learn How to Cook Healthy and Delicious Meals Easily with Your Air Fryer on a Budget

Linda Wang

© **Copyright 2021 by Linda Wang - All rights reserved.**

The content contained within this book may not be reproduced, duplicated or transmitted without direct written permission from the author or the publisher.
Under no circumstances will any blame or legal responsibility be held against the publisher, or author, for any damages, reparation, or monetary loss due to the information contained within this book. Either directly or indirectly.

Legal Notice:
This book is copyright protected. This book is only for personal use. You cannot amend, distribute, sell, use, quote or paraphrase any part, or the content within this book, without the consent of the author or publisher.

Disclaimer Notice:
Please note the information contained within this document is for educational and entertainment purposes only. All effort has been executed to present accurate, up to date, and reliable, complete information. No warranties of any kind are declared or implied. Readers acknowledge that the author is not engaging in the rendering of legal, financial, medical or professional advice. The content within this book has been derived from various sources. Please consult a licensed professional before attempting any techniques outlined in this book.
By reading this document, the reader agrees that under no circumstances is the author responsible for any losses, direct or indirect, which are incurred as a result of the use of information contained within this document, including, but not limited to, — errors, omissions, or inaccuracies.

TABLE OF CONTENTS

INTRODUCTION 1

Breakfast Pockets 5

Air Fryer Bacon 8

Air Fryer Breakfast Bake 10

Corn Pudding 12

Delicious Meatloaf with Black Peppercorns 14

Simple Cheese Wraps 16

Special Mac and Cheese 17

Sausage Mushroom Caps 19

Zucchini and Peppers with Saucy Sweet Potatoes 21

Yummy Potatoes Gratin 23

Shrimp Scampi 25

Lemon Shrimp 29

Lemony Tuna 27

Haddock with Cheese Sauce 29

Roasted Red Snapper 33

Fish Tacos 35

Chicken with Apple 37

Chicken with Yogurt and Mustard 39

Tandoori Chicken 41

Balsamic Chicken 43

Spicy Buffalo Wings	45
Sweet Mustard Chicken	47
Spiced Lamb Steaks	48
Lamb Ribs	50
Beef and Peas	52
Delicious Sausage	54
Saltimbocca Roman Veal	55
Cinnamon Pork Rinds	57
Glazed Veggies	59
Delightful Mushrooms	61
Parmesan Asparagus	63
Air fryer Vegetable Soup	65
Creamy Cauliflower Soup	67
Taco Cheese Soup	69
Asian Pork Soup	71
Sweet & Spicy Cauliflower	73
Butterflied Chicken with Herbs	75
4-Ingredient Garlic Herb Chicken Wings	78
Crab and Artichoke Dip	79
Simple & Delicious Spiced Apples	81
Plum Cream	83
Yogurt Cake	84
Dark Chocolate Cake	86

Ninja Pop-Tarts 88

Coconut Donuts 91

Strawberry Jam 93

Amaretto Cream 94

Keto-Friendly Doughnut Recipe 95

Pear Pastry Pouch 97

Chocolate Chip Pan Cookie 99

NOTES 101

INTRODUCTION

An Air Fryer is a magic revolutionized kitchen appliance that helps you fry with less or even no oil at all. This kind of product applies Rapid Air technology, which offers a new way to fry with less oil. This new invention cooks food through the circulation of superheated air and generates 80% low-fat food. Although the food is fried with less oil, you don't need to worry as the food processed by the Air Fryer still has the same taste like the food fried using the deep-frying method.

This technology uses a superheated element, which radiates heat close to the food and an exhaust fan in its lid to circulate airflow. An Air Fryer ensures that the food processed is cooked completely. The exhaust fan located at the top of the cooking chamber helps the food get the same heating temperature in every part quickly, resulting in a cooked food of better and healthier quality. Besides, cooking with an Air Fryer is also suitable for those individuals which are too busy or do not have enough time. For example, an Air Fryer only needs half a spoonful of oil and takes 10 minutes to serve a medium bowl of crispy French fries.

In addition to serving healthier food, an Air Fryer also provides some other benefits to you. Since an Air Fryer helps you fry using less oil or without oil for some kind of food, it automatically reduces the fat and cholesterol content in food. Indeed, no one will refuse to enjoy fried food without worrying about the greasy and fat content. Having fried food with no guilt is one of the pleasures of life. Besides having low fat and cholesterol, you save some amount of money by consuming oil sparingly, which can be used for other needs. An Air Fryer also can reheat your food. Sometimes, when you have fried leftover and you reheat it, it will usually serve reheated greasy food with some addition of unhealthy reuse oil. Undoubtedly, the saturated fat in the fried food gets worse because of this process. An Air Fryer helps you reheat your food without being afraid of extra oils that the food may absorb. Fried bananas, fish and chips, nuggets, or even fried chicken can be reheated to become as warm and crispy as they were before by using an Air Fryer.

Some people may think that spending some amount of money to buy a fryer is wasteful. I dare to say that they are wrong because an Air Fryer is not only used to fry. It is a sophisticated multi-function appliance since it also helps you to roast chicken, make steak, grill fish, and even bake a cake. With a built-in air filter, an Air Fryer filters the air and saves your kitchen from smoke and grease.

An air Fryer is really a new innovative method of cooking. Grab it fast and welcome to a clean and healthy kitchen.

Breakfast Pockets

Preparation Time: 15 minutes

Cooking Time: 30 minutes

Servings: 4

Ingredients:

- 2 sheets: 17.25 oz. almond flour puff pastry, cut into 4 equal sized pieces

- 2 eggs, lightly beaten
- 1 package: 6 oz. ground breakfast sausage, crumbled
- 1 cup cheddar cheese, shredded
- ½ teaspoon ground black pepper
- 1 teaspoon kosher salt
- 2 tablespoons canola oil

Directions:

1. Preheat the Air fryer to 375 degrees F and grease the Air fryer basket.
2. Arrange the sausages in the basket and roast for about 15 minutes.
3. Place the eggs into the basket and cook for about 5 minutes.
4. Season with salt and black pepper and divide the egg sausage mixture over the 4 puff pastry rectangles.
5. Top with shredded cheddar cheese and drizzle with canola oil.
6. Place 1 egg pocket in the basket and cook for 6 minutes at 400 degree F.

7. Remove from the Air fryer and repeat with the remaining pockets.
8. Serve warm and enjoy.

Nutrition:

Calories: 197, Fats: 15.4g, Carbs: 8.5g, Sugar: 1.1g, Proteins: 7.9g, Sodium: 203mg

Air Fryer Bacon

Preparation Time: 1 minutes

Cooking Time: 9 minutes

Servings: 6

Ingredients:

- ½ tablespoon olive oil
- 6 bacon strips
-

Directions:

1. Preheat the Air fryer to 350 degrees F and grease an Air fryer basket with olive oil.
2. Cook for about 9 minutes and flip the bacon.
3. Cook for 3 more minutes until crispy and serve warm.

Nutrition:

Calories: 245, Fat: 17.1g, Carbohydrates: 10.2g, Sugar: 2.7g, Protein: 12.8g, Sodium: 580mg

Air Fryer Breakfast Bake

Preparation Time: 15 minutes

Cooking Time: 25 minutes

Servings: 2

Ingredients:

- 4 eggs
- 1½ cups baby spinach
- 1 slice whole grain bread, torn into pieces
- 1/3 cup cheddar cheese, shredded
- ½ teaspoon kosher salt
- ½ cup bell pepper, diced
- 1 teaspoon hot sauce

Directions:

1. Preheat the Air fryer to 250 degrees F and grease a 6-inch soufflé dish with nonstick cooking spray.
2. Whisk together eggs, salt and hot sauce in a bowl.

3. Dip the bread pieces, spinach, ¼ cup cheddar cheese and bell pepper in the whisked eggs.
4. Pour this mixture into the prepared soufflé dish and sprinkle with the remaining cheese.
5. Transfer into the Air fryer basket and cook for about 25 minutes.
6. Remove from the Air fryer basket and let it rest for 10 minutes before serving.

Nutrition:

Calories: 249, Fat: 15.7g, Carbohydrates: 10.3g, Sugar: 3.4g, Protein: 18.2g, Sodium: 979mg

Corn Pudding

Preparation Time: 1 hour 25 minutes

Servings: 6

Ingredients:

- 4 bacon slices; cooked and chopped.
- 3 cups bread; cubed
- 3 eggs
- 1/2 cup heavy cream
- 1½ cups whole milk
- 2 cups corn
- 1 cup cheddar cheese; grated
- 1/2 cup green bell pepper; chopped
- 1 yellow onion; chopped.
- 1/4 cup celery; chopped.
- 2 tsp. garlic; grated
- 1 tsp. thyme; chopped.
- 3 tbsp. parmesan cheese; grated
- 1 tbsp. olive oil
- Salt and black pepper

Directions:

1. Heat up the oil in a pan over medium heat. Add the corn, celery, onion, bell pepper, salt, pepper, garlic and thyme to the pan; stir, sauté for 15 minutes and transfer to a bowl
2. To the same bowl, add the bacon, milk, cream, eggs, salt, pepper, bread and cheddar cheese. Stir well, then pour into a casserole dish that fits your air fryer
3. Place the dish in the fryer and cook at 350°F for 30 minutes
4. Sprinkle the pudding with parmesan cheese and cook for 30 minutes more. Slice, divide between plates and serve.

Delicious Meatloaf with Black Peppercorns

Preparation Time: 55 minutes

Servings: 2

Ingredients:

- 4 Pounds beef [minced]
- 1 onion [large; diced]

- 1 teaspoon Worcester sauce
- 3 tablespoon tomato ketchup
- 1 tablespoon oregano
- 1 tablespoon parsley
- 1 tablespoon basil
- 1 tablespoon mixed herbs
- pepper to taste
- 3 tablespoon breadcrumbs
- salt according to taste

Directions:

1. Put the beef mince in a bowl and mix it with onion, herbs, ketchup and Worcester sauce. Stir well.
2. Add breadcrumbs to the mixture.
3. Put the seasoned beef in a dish and put in Air Fryer. Cook for 25 minutes at 390 - degrees Fahrenheit.
4. Serve with rice or mashed potatoes.

Simple Cheese Wraps

Preparation Time: 35 minutes

Servings: 2

Ingredients:

- 1/2-pound cheese [provolone; diced]
- 1 pack egg roll wrapper
- 1 steak [frozen; sliced]
- 1 onion; chopped
- 1 bell pepper [green; chopped]
- salt and pepper to taste

Directions:

1. Sauté onion and bell pepper for 5 minutes. Cook the steak, then shred it.
2. Mix these with cheese. Fill the wrappers and roll them.
3. Air fry for 5 min at 350 degrees Fahrenheit; then raise temp to 392 degrees Fahrenheit and fry for 5 minutes.
4. The meal is ready to be served. Enjoy the taste.

Special Mac and Cheese

Preparation Time: 25 minutes

Servings: 2

Ingredients:

- 1 cup elbow macaroni
- 1/2 cup milk; warmed
- 1/2 cup broccoli or cauliflower; chopped
- 1 ½ cups cheddar cheese; grated

- 1 tablespoon parmesan; grated
- salt and pepper to taste

Directions:

1. Bring a medium pot of water to a boil and add the macaroni and vegetables.
2. Cook until just tender; 7 – 10 minutes, and drain.
3. Toss the still-hot macaroni and vegetables with the milk and cheddar and transfer to a baking dish. Season with salt and pepper.
4. Briefly preheat your Air Fryer to 350 - degrees Fahrenheit.
5. Sprinkle the macaroni with the parmesan and bake until bubbling; about 15 minutes.
6. Let cool slightly before serving.

Sausage Mushroom Caps

Preparation Time: 18 minutes

Servings: 2

Ingredients:

- ½ lb. Italian sausage
- ¼ cup grated Parmesan cheese.
- 6 large Portobello mushroom caps
- ¼ cup chopped onion
- 1 tsp. minced fresh garlic
- 2 tbsp. blanched finely ground almond flour

Directions:

1. Use a spoon to hollow out each mushroom cap, reserving scrapings.
2. In a medium skillet over medium heat, brown the sausage about 10 minutes or until fully cooked and no pink remains. Drain and then add reserved mushroom scrapings, onion, almond flour, Parmesan and garlic.

3. Gently fold ingredients together and continue cooking an additional minute, then remove from heat
4. Evenly spoon the mixture into mushroom caps and place the caps into a 6-inch round pan. Place pan into the air fryer basket
5. Adjust the temperature to 375 Degrees F and set the timer for 8 minutes. When finished cooking, the tops will be browned and bubbling. Serve warm.

Nutrition:

Calories: 404; Protein: 24.3g; Fiber: 4.5g; Fat: 25.8g; Carbs: 18.2g

Zucchini and Peppers with Saucy Sweet Potatoes

Preparation Time: 20 minutes

Servings: 4

Ingredients:

- 2 large-sized sweet potatoes; peeled and quartered
- 1 Serrano pepper; deveined and thinly sliced
- 1 medium-sized zucchini; sliced
- 1 bell pepper; deveined and thinly sliced
- 1/4 cup olive oil
- 1 – 2 carrots; cut into matchsticks
- 1 ½ tablespoon maple syrup
- 1/2 teaspoon porcini powder
- 1/2 teaspoon fennel seeds
- 1/4 teaspoon mustard powder
- 1 tablespoon garlic powder
- 1/2 teaspoon fine sea salt
- 1/4 teaspoon ground black pepper

- Tomato ketchup; to serve

Directions:

1. Place the sweet potatoes, zucchini, peppers, and the carrot into the Air Fryer cooking basket.
2. Drizzle with olive oil and toss to coat, cook in the preheated machine at 350 - degrees Fahrenheit for 15 minutes.
3. While the vegetables are cooking, prepare the sauce by thoroughly whisking the other ingredients, without the tomato ketchup.
4. Lightly grease a baking dish that fits into your machine.
5. Transfer cooked vegetables to the prepared baking dish; add the sauce and toss to coat well.
6. Turn the machine to 390 - degrees Fahrenheit and cook the vegetables for 5 more minutes.
7. Serve warm with tomato ketchup on the side.

Yummy Potatoes Gratin

Preparation Time: 55 minutes

Servings: 3

Ingredients:

- 7 medium russet potatoes; peeled
- 1/2 cup cream
- 1/2 cup milk
- 1 teaspoon black pepper
- 1/2 cup Gruyère or semi-mature cheese; grated
- 1/2 teaspoon nutmeg

Directions:

1. Preheat the Air Fryer to 390 - degrees Fahrenheit.
2. Slice the potatoes wafer-thin. In a bowl, mix the milk and cream and season to taste with salt, pepper and nutmeg.
3. Coat the potato slices with the milk mixture.

4. Transfer the potato slices to 8-inch heat-resistant baking dish and pour the rest of the cream mixture from the bowl on top of the potatoes.
5. Place the baking dish in the cooking basket into the Air Fryer.
6. Set the timer and cook for 25 minutes. Remove the cooking basket and distribute the cheese evenly over the potatoes.
7. Set the timer for 10 minutes and bake the gratin until it is nicely browned.
8. Tips: Instead of milk, you can substitute two eggs

Shrimp Scampi

Preparation Time: 10 minutes

Cooking Time: 10 minutes

Serve: 4

Ingredients:

- 1 lb shrimp, peeled and deveined
- 2 tbsp olive oil
- 10 garlic cloves, peeled

- 1 fresh lemon, cut into wedges
- 1/4 cup parmesan cheese, grated
- 2 tbsp butter, melted

Directions:

1. Preheat the air fryer to 370 F.
2. Mix together shrimp, lemon wedges, olive oil, and garlic cloves in a bowl.
3. Pour shrimp mixture into the air fryer pan and place into the air fryer and cook for 10 minutes.
4. Drizzle with melted butter and sprinkle with parmesan cheese.
5. Serve and enjoy.

Nutrition:

Calories 295, Fat 17 g, Carbohydrates 4 g, Sugar 0.1 g, Protein 29 g, Cholesterol 260 mg

Lemony Tuna

Preparation Time: 15 minutes

Cooking Time: 12 minutes

Servings: 8

Ingredients:

- 4 tablespoons fresh parsley, chopped
- 1 cup breadcrumbs
- 4: 6-ouncecans water packed plain tuna
- 2 eggs
- 2 tablespoons fresh lime juice
- 4 teaspoons Dijon mustard
- 6 tablespoons canola oil
- Dash of hot sauce
- Salt and black pepper, to taste

Directions:

1. Preheat the Air fryer to 360 degree F and grease an Air fryer basket.

2. Mix tuna fish, breadcrumbs, mustard, parsley, hot sauce, canola oil, eggs, salt and lime juice in a large bowl.
3. Make equal-sized patties from the mixture and refrigerate for about 3 hours.
4. Transfer the patties into the Air fryer basket and cook for about 12 minutes.
5. Dish out and serve warm.

Nutrition:

Calories: 388, Fat: 21.8g, Carbohydrates: 31.7g, Sugar: 1.2g, Protein: 14.2g, Sodium: 680mg

Lemon Shrimp

Preparation Time: 10 minutes

Cooking Time: 8 minutes

Serve: 2

Ingredients:

- 12 oz shrimp, peeled and deveined
- 1/4 tsp garlic powder
- 1 lemon sliced

- 1/4 tsp paprika
- 1 tsp lemon pepper
- 1 tbsp olive oil
- 1 lemon juice

Directions:

1. In a bowl, mix together oil, lemon juice, garlic powder, paprika, and lemon pepper.
2. Add shrimp to the bowl and toss well to coat.
3. Spray air fryer basket with cooking spray.
4. Transfer shrimp into the air fryer basket and cook at 400 °F for 8 minutes.
5. Garnish with lemon slices and serve.

Nutrition:

Calories 381, Fat 17.1 g, Carbohydrates 4.1 g, Sugar 0.6 g, Protein 50.6 g, Cholesterol 358 mg

Haddock with Cheese Sauce

Preparation Time: 15 minutes

Cooking Time: 8 minutes

Servings: 4

Ingredients:

- 4: 6-ouncehaddock fillets
- 4 tablespoons pine nuts
- 6 tablespoons fresh basil, chopped

- 2 tablespoons Parmesan cheese, grated
- 2 tablespoons olive oil
- Salt and black pepper, to taste

Directions:

1. Preheat the Air fryer to 360 degrees F and grease an Air fryer basket.
2. Season the haddock fillets with salt and black pepper and coat evenly with olive oil.
3. Transfer the haddock fillets in the Air fryer basket and cook for about 8 minutes.
4. Meanwhile, put the rest of the ingredients in a food processor and pulse until smooth to make the cheese sauce.
5. Dish out the haddock fillets in the bowl and top with cheese sauce to serve.

Nutrition:

Calories: 354, Fat: 17.5g, Carbohydrates: 1.7g, Sugar: 0.3g, Protein: 47g, Sodium: 278mg

Roasted Red Snapper

Preparation Time: 20 minutes

Servings: 4

Ingredients:

- 4 red snapper fillets; boneless
- 2 garlic cloves; minced
- 1 tbsp. hot chili paste

- 2 tbsp. olive oil
- 2 tbsp. coconut aminos
- 2 tbsp. lime juice
- A pinch of salt and black pepper

Directions:

1. Take a bowl and mix all the ingredients except the fish and whisk well
2. Rub the fish with this mix, place it in your air fryer's basket and cook at 380°F for 15 minutes
3. Serve with a side salad.

Nutrition:

Calories: 220; Fat: 13g; Fiber: 4g; Carbs: 6g; Protein: 11g

Fish Tacos

Preparation time: 20 minutes

Servings: 6

Ingredients:

- Tempura batter: 1 cup made from:
- Cornstarch: 1 tbsp.
- Flour: 1 cup

- Cold seltzer water: .5 cup
- Coleslaw: 1 cup
- Salsa: .5 cup
- White pepper: 1 tsp.
- Chopped cilantro: 2 tbsp.
- Guacamole: .5 cup
- Lemon wedges: 1
- Salt & pepper: 1 pinch each

Directions:
1. Prep the tempura batter using salt, pepper. cornstarch, and flour.
2. Slice the cod into two-ounce pieces: 6 pieces and sprinkle using the salt and pepper.
3. Use the batter to coat the cod. Dredge them in the panko.
4. Use the French fry setting and set the timer for ten minutes. Turn after five minutes.
5. Top each portion with coleslaw, salsa, guacamole, cilantro, or lemon juice.

Chicken with Apple

Preparation Time: 10 minutes

Cooking Time: 20 minutes

Servings: 8

Ingredients:

- 1 shallot, thinly sliced
- 2: 4-ouncesboneless, skinless chicken thighs, sliced into chunks
- 1 teaspoon fresh thyme, minced
- 1 large apple, cored and cubed
- 1 tablespoon fresh ginger, finely grated
- 2 tablespoons maple syrup
- ½ cup apple cider
- Salt and black pepper, as required

Directions:

1. Preheat the Air fryer to 390 degrees F and grease an Air fryer basket.

2. Mix the shallot, ginger, thyme, apple cider, maple syrup, salt, and black pepper in a bowl.
3. Coat the chicken generously with the marinade and refrigerate to marinate for about 8 hours.
4. Arrange the chicken pieces and cubed apples into the Air Fryer basket and cook for about 20 minutes, flipping once halfway.
5. Dish out the chicken mixture into a serving bowl to serve.

Nutrition:

Calories: 299, Fat: 26.2g, Carbohydrates: 39.9g, Sugar: 30.4g, Protein: 26.2g, Sodium: 125mg

Chicken with Yogurt and Mustard

Preparation time: 10 - 20,

Cooking time: 15 – 30;

Serve: 6

Ingredients:

- 500 g chicken breast
- 40 g mustard
- 100 g of white yogurt
- 1 shallot
- Pepper to taste
- Salt to taste

Direction:

1. Place the chopped shallot inside the basket previously greased.
2. Brown for 3 minutes at 150 °C
3. Add the chicken pieces, salt, pepper and cook for another 15 minutes at 180°C.

4. Then pour the mustard and yogurt and cook for another 5 minutes.

Nutrition:

Calories 287.1, Fat 8.9g, Carbohydrate 4.3 g, Sugars 1.7 g, Protein43.6 g, Cholesterol 99.9 mg

Tandoori Chicken

Preparation time: more than 30,

Cooking time: 15 – 30;

Serve: 4

Ingredients:

- 600 g chicken pieces
- 125 g whole yogurt
- 3 tsp of spices for roasted meats

- 1 tbsp curry

Direction:

1. Place all ingredients in a bowl, flame well and let stand for 1 hour in the refrigerator.
2. Place the pieces of meat in the basket and set the temperature to 160 °C
3. Cook the meat for 30 minutes, turning it 1-2 times to brown the chicken on both sides.

Nutrition:

Calories 263, Fat 12g, Carbohydrates 6.1g, Sugars 3.7g, Protein 31g, Cholesterol 135mg

Balsamic Chicken

Preparation Time: 30 minutes

Servings: 4

Ingredients:

- 4 chicken breasts; skinless and boneless
- 1/4 cup cheddar cheese; grated
- 1 yellow onion; minced
- 1/4 tsp. garlic powder
- 1/4 cup balsamic vinegar
- 12 oz. canned tomatoes; chopped.
- Salt and black pepper to taste

Directions:

1. In a baking dish that fits your air fryer, mix the chicken with the onions, vinegar, tomatoes, salt, pepper and garlic powder
2. Sprinkle the cheese on top and place the pan in the air fryer; cook at 400°F for 20 minutes. Divide between plates and serve.

Spicy Buffalo Wings

Cooking Time: 26 minutes

Servings: 4

Ingredients:

- 2 lbs. chicken wings
- 1/2 cup hot & spicy sauce; divided
- 6 tbsp. melted butter; divided
- Salt to taste

Directions:

1. In a bowl, mix ¼ cup hot and spicy sauce and 3 tbsp. of melted butter. Cover chicken pieces with the mixture and marinate for 2 hours in the fridge
2. Preheat your air fryer to 400°F. Split the wings into 2 batches. Place the first batch into air fryer and cook for 12 minutes, shaking halfway through cook time
3. Repeat with the second batch. Place all the wings into air fryer for an additional 2 minute cooking time.
4. Finish preparing sauce by mixing the remaining 3 tbsp. of butter and ¼ cup of hot sauce. Dip cooked wings in sauce and enjoy!

Sweet Mustard Chicken

Cooking Time: 12 minutes

Servings: 4

Ingredients:

- 12 oz. chicken breast; diced
- 6 oz. Sweet Mustard sauce
- 1 cup cornstarch
- 1/4 cup milk
- 1/2 tsp. white pepper

Directions:

1. Add milk and chicken to a mixing bowl and set aside for 2 minutes. Drain the milk from the chicken and toss chicken with cornstarch
2. Place the chicken in the air fryer at 350°F for 12 minutes. Place chicken in the serving dish and sprinkle with white pepper along with a dish of sauce for dipping chicken pieces in.

Spiced Lamb Steaks

Preparation Time: 15 minutes

Cooking Time: 15 minutes

Servings: 3

Ingredients:

- ½ onion, roughly chopped
- 1½ pounds boneless lamb sirloin steaks
- 1 tablespoon fresh ginger, peeled
- 5 garlic cloves, peeled
- 1 teaspoon garam masala
- ½ teaspoon ground cumin
- 1 teaspoon ground fennel
- ½ teaspoon ground cinnamon
- ½ teaspoon cayenne pepper
- Salt and black pepper, to taste

Directions:

1. Preheat the Air fryer to 330 degrees F and grease an Air fryer basket.

2. Put the onion, garlic, ginger, and spices in a blender and pulse until smooth.
3. Coat the lamb steaks with this mixture on both sides and refrigerate to marinate for about 24 hours.
4. Arrange the lamb steaks in the Air fryer basket and cook for about 15 minutes, flipping once in between.
5. Dish out the steaks in a platter and serve warm.

Nutrition:

Calories: 252, Fat: 16.7g, Carbohydrates: 4.2g, Sugar: 0.7g, Protein: 21.7g, Sodium: 42mg

Lamb Ribs

Preparation Time: 20 minutes

Servings: 4

Ingredients:

- 4 lamb ribs
- 1/4 tsp. smoked paprika
- 1 cup veggie stock

- 1/2 tsp. chili powder
- 4 garlic cloves; minced
- 2 tbsp. extra virgin olive oil
- Salt and black pepper to taste

Directions:

1. In a bowl, combine all of the ingredients except the ribs and mix well.
2. Then add the ribs and rub them thoroughly with the mixture
3. Transfer the ribs to your air fryer's basket and cook at 390 °F for 7 minutes on each side. Serve with a side salad

Beef and Peas

Preparation Time: 25 minutes

Servings: 2

Ingredients:

- 2 beef steaks; cut into strips
- 1 tbsp. olive oil
- 2 tbsp. soy sauce

- 14 oz. snow peas
- Salt and black pepper to taste

Directions:

1. Put all of the ingredients into a pan that fits your air fryer; toss well.
2. Place the pan in the fryer and cook at 390 °F for 25 minutes. Divide everything between plates and serve

Delicious Sausage

Preparation Time: 25 minutes

Servings: 4

Ingredients:

- 6 pork sausage links; halved
- 1 tbsp. olive oil
- 1 red onion; sliced
- 1 tbsp. rosemary; chopped.
- 1 tbsp. sweet paprika
- 2 garlic cloves; minced
- Salt and black pepper to taste

Directions:

1. In a pan that fits your air fryer, mix all of the ingredients and toss.
2. Place the pan in the fryer and cook at 360 °F for 20 minutes. Divide between plates and serve

Saltimbocca Roman Veal

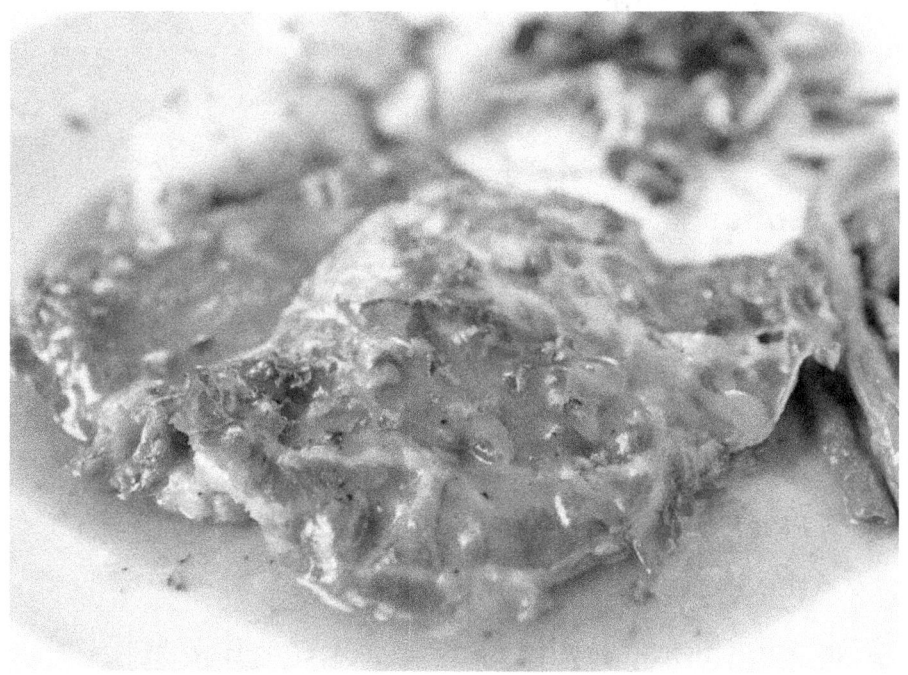

Preparation time: 10 minutes,

Cooking time: 15 minutes;

Serve: 4

Ingredients

- 70-80 g See
- 16 slices of raw ham

- 20 g butter
- 16 sage leaves
- Pepper to taste
- Salt to taste

Directions:

1. Place the meat slices on a sheet of parchment paper. Arrange the ham slices on the meat, put the washed sage leaf, roll, and close with a toothpick.
2. Place the butter in the basket at 150 °C. Melt the butter for 2 min.
3. Add the meat and simmer for 6 minutes.

Nutrition:

Calories 323, Fat 18g, Carbohydrates 1.7g, Sugars 0.4g, Protein 29g, Cholesterol 124mg

Cinnamon Pork Rinds

Preparation Time: 10 minutes

Servings: 2

Ingredients:

- 2 oz. pork rinds
- 2 tbsp. unsalted butter; melted.
- ¼ cup powdered erythritol
- ½ tsp. ground cinnamon.

Directions:

1. Take a large bowl, toss pork rinds and butter. Sprinkle with cinnamon and erythritol, then toss to coat evenly.
2. Place pork rinds into the air fryer basket. Adjust the temperature to 400 Degrees F and set the timer for 5 minutes. Serve immediately.

Nutrition:

Calories: 264; Protein: 16.3g; Fiber: 0.4g; Fat: 20.8g; Carbs: 18.5g

Glazed Veggies

Preparation Time: 20 minutes

Cooking Time: 20 minutes

Servings: 4

Ingredients:

- 2 ounces cherry tomatoes
- 1 large carrot, peeled and chopped
- 1 large parsnip, peeled and chopped
- 1 large zucchini, chopped
- 6 tablespoons olive oil, divided
- 1 green bell pepper, seeded and chopped
- 3 tablespoons honey
- 1 teaspoon Dijon mustard
- 1 teaspoon garlic paste
- 1 teaspoon mixed dried herbs
- Salt and black pepper, to taste

Directions:

1. Preheat the Air fryer to 350 degree F and grease an Air fryer pan.
2. Arrange cherry tomatoes, parsnip, carrot, zucchini and bell pepper in the Air fryer pan and drizzle with 3 tablespoons of olive oil.
3. Cook for about 15 minutes and remove from the Air fryer.
4. Mix remaining olive oil, honey, mustard, herbs, garlic, salt, and black pepper in a bowl.
5. Pour this mixture over the vegetables in the Air fryer pan and set the Air fryer to 390 degree F.
6. Cook for about 5 minutes and dish out to serve hot.

Nutrition:

Calories: 288, Fat: 21.4g, Carbohydrates: 26.7g, Sugar: 18.7g, Protein: 2.1g, Sodium: 79mg

Delightful Mushrooms

Preparation Time: 20 minutes

Cooking Time: 22 minutes

Servings: 4

Ingredients:

- 2 cups mushrooms, sliced
- 1 tablespoon fresh chives, chopped
- 2 tablespoons cheddar cheese, shredded

- 2 tablespoons olive oil

Directions:

1. Preheat the Air fryer to 355 degrees F and grease an Air fryer basket.
2. Coat the mushrooms with olive oil and arrange into the Air fryer basket.
3. Cook for about 20 minutes and dish out in a platter.
4. Top with chives and cheddar cheese and cook for 2 more minutes.
5. Dish out and serve warm.

Nutrition:

Calories: 218, Fat: 7.9g, Carbohydrates: 33.6g, Sugar: 2.5g, Protein: 4.6g, Sodium: 55mg

Parmesan Asparagus

Servings: 3

Preparation Time: 15 minutes

Cooking Time: 10 minutes

Ingredients

- 1 pound fresh asparagus, trimmed
- 1 tablespoon Parmesan cheese, grated
- 1 tablespoon butter, melted
- 1 teaspoon garlic powder
- Salt and ground black pepper, as required

Directions:

1. In a bowl, mix together the asparagus, cheese, butter, garlic powder, salt, and black pepper.
2. Set the temperature of air fryer to 400 degrees F. Grease an air fryer basket.
3. Arrange asparagus into the prepared air fryer basket.
4. Air fry for about 10 minutes.

5. Remove from air fryer and transfer the asparagus onto serving plates.
6. Serve hot.

Nutrition:

Calories: 73, Carbohydrate: 6.6g, Protein: 4.2g, Fat: 2.7g, Sugar: 3.1g, Sodium: 95mg

Air fryer Vegetable Soup

Preparation Time: 10 minutes

Cooking Time: 20 minutes

Servings: 5

Ingredients:

- 2 tablespoons extra virgin olive oil
- ½ green bell pepper, chopped
- ½ onion, chopped
- 2 cloves garlic, minced
- 1 1/2 cups small cauliflower florets
- 1 1/2 cups green cabbage, chopped
- 1 cup chopped carrots
- ½ cup green beans, cut into small pieces
- 1 can diced tomatoes, no salt added
- 4 cups low-sodium vegetable broth
- 1 bay leaf
- ½ teaspoon salt
- 15-ounce cannellini beans, rinsed
- 4 cups of chopped spinach
- ¼ cup chopped basil

Directions:

1. Place olive oil in the air fryer and set to saute. Add onions, bell peppers, and garlic, then cook, often stirring until starting to soften, which will take 2-3 minutes.
2. Put in the carrots, cauliflower, cabbage, and green beans and cook for 4-5 minutes, stirring often.
3. Add the broth, tomatoes, bay leaf, and salt. Turn off the heat, lock the lid, and cook on high for 5 minutes.
4. Release the pressure using quick release, open the lid carefully, and remove bay leaf. Stir in the spinach, basil, and beans.
5. Ready to serve. May drizzle more olive oil on top if desired.

Nutrition:

Calories – 192 Protein – 7.3 g. Fat – 6.6 g. Carbs – 26 g.

Creamy Cauliflower Soup

Preparation Time: 10 minutes

Cooking Time: 32 minutes

Servings: 4

Ingredients:

- 2 cups cauliflower florets
- 5 cups chicken broth
- 1 tsp. pumpkin pie spice
- 3 tbsp. olive oil
- 1 onion, chopped
- ¼ tsp. salt

Directions:

1. Add oil into air fryer and set on Sauté mode.
2. Add onion to the pot and sauté for 5 minutes.
3. Add cauliflower and cook for a minute. Add broth and season with sea salt.
4. Secure pot with lid and cook on manual high pressure for 24 minutes.

5. Quickly release the pressure then open the lid.
6. Puree the soup using an immersion blender until smooth.
7. Add pumpkin pie spice and stir well. Cook on Sauté mode for 2 minutes.
8. Serve and enjoy.

Nutrition:

Calories – 163 Protein – 7.4 g. Fat – 12.3 g. Carbs – 6.7 g.

Taco Cheese Soup

Preparation Time: 10 minutes

Cooking Time: 25 minutes

Servings: 8

Ingredients:
- 1 lb. ground beef
- 1 lb. ground pork
- 2 tbsp. parsley, chopped
- ½ cup Monterey Jack cheese, grated
- 4 cups beef broth
- 16 oz. cream cheese
- 20 oz. can tomatoes
- 2 tbsp. taco seasonings

Directions:
1. Add both the ground meats in the air fryer and sauté for 10 minutes.
2. Add taco seasonings, tomatoes and cream cheese. Stir to combine.

3. Secure pot with lid and cook on manual high pressure for 15 minutes.
4. Quickly release the pressure then open the lid.
5. Add parsley and stir well. Top with grated cheese and serve.

Nutrition:

Calories – 445 Protein – 41.1 g. Fat – 28.1 g. Carbs – 5.7 g.

Asian Pork Soup

Preparation Time: 10 minutes

Cooking Time: 30 minutes

Servings: 5

Ingredients:

- 1 lb. ground pork
- 1 tsp. ground ginger
- 4 cups beef broth
- ¼ cup soy sauce
- ½ cabbage head, chopped
- 2 carrots, peeled and shredded
- 1 tbsp. olive oil
- 1 onion, chopped
- Pepper
- Salt

Directions:

1. Add oil into air fryer and set on Sauté mode.
2. Add meat to the pot and sauté for 5 minutes.

3. Add remaining ingredients and stir well.
4. Secure pot with lid and cook on manual high pressure for 25 minutes.
5. Quick release pressure then open the lid.
6. Stir well and serve hot.

Nutrition:

Calories – 229 Protein – 29.8 g. Fat – 7.2 g. Carbs – 10.6 g.

Sweet & Spicy Cauliflower

Servings: 4

Preparation Time: 15 minutes

Cooking Time: 30 minutes

Ingredients

- 1 head cauliflower, cut into florets
- ¾ cup onion, thinly sliced
- 1½ tablespoons soy sauce
- 5 garlic cloves, finely sliced
- 1 tablespoon hot sauce
- 1 teaspoon coconut sugar
- 1 tablespoon rice vinegar
- Pinch of red pepper flakes
- Ground black pepper, as required
- 2 scallions, chopped

Directions:

1. Set the temperature of air fryer to 350 degrees F. Grease an air fryer pan.

2. Arrange cauliflower florets into the prepared air fryer pan in a single layer.
3. Air fry for about 10 minutes.
4. Remove from air fryer and stir in the onions.
5. Air fry for another 10 minutes.
6. Remove from air fryer and stir in the garlic.
7. Air fry for 5 more minutes.
8. Meanwhile, in a bowl, mix well soy sauce, hot sauce, vinegar, coconut sugar, red pepper flakes, and black pepper.
9. Remove from the air fryer and stir in the sauce mixture.
10. Air fry for about 5 minutes.
11. Remove from air fryer and transfer the cauliflower mixture onto serving plates.
12. Garnish with scallions and serve.

Nutrition:

Calories: 72, Carbohydrate: 13.8g, Protein: 3.6g, Fat: 0.2g, Sugar: 3.1g, Sodium: 1300mg

Butterflied Chicken with Herbs

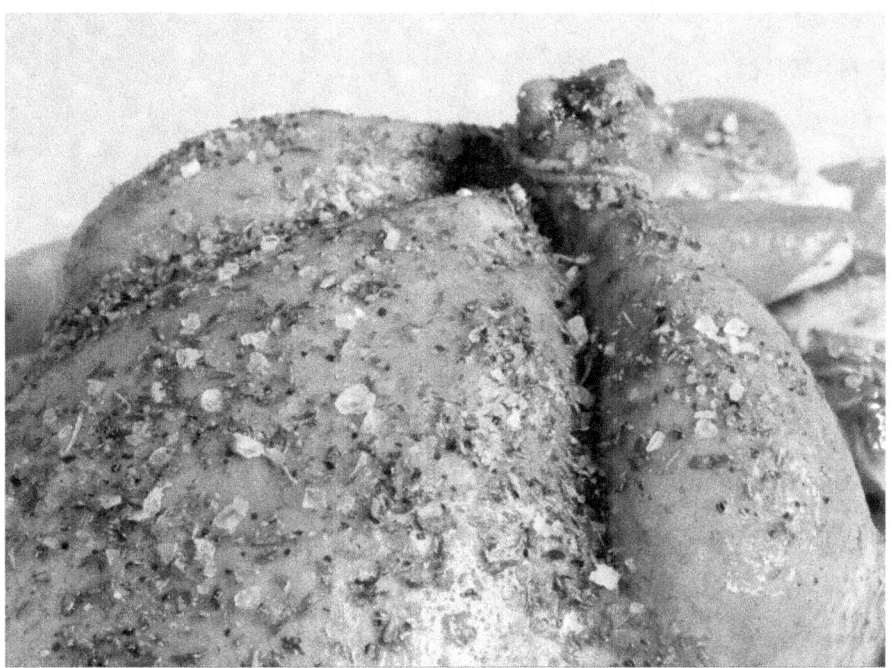

Servings: 4

Cooking Time: 1 hour

Ingredients:

- 2 pounds whole chicken, backbones removed and butterflied
- 6 cloves of garlic, minced

- ¼ cup Aleppo-style pepper
- ¼ cup fresh lemon juice
- 1 and 1/4 cup chopped rosemary
- ¼ cup oregano
- 1 cup green olives, pitted and cracked
- Salt and pepper to taste

Directions

1. Place the chicken breast side up and slice through the breasts. Using your palms, press against the breastbone to flatten the breasts or you may remove the bones altogether.
2. Once the bones have been removed, season the chicken with salt, pepper, garlic, pepper, rosemary, lemon juice, and oregano.
3. Allow marinating in the fridge for at least 12 hours.
4. Preheat the air fryer at 375 degrees F.
5. Place the grill pan accessory in the air fryer.
6. Place the chicken on the grill pan and place the olives around the chicken.

7. Grill for 1 hour and make sure to flip the chicken every 10 minutes for even grilling.

Nutrition

Calories: 492; Carbs:50.4 g; Protein:37.6 g; Fat: 16.6g

4-Ingredient Garlic Herb Chicken Wings

Servings: 4

Cooking Time: 35 minutes

Ingredients:

- 2 pounds chicken wings
- ¼ cup chopped rosemary
- 6 medium garlic cloves, grated
- Salt and pepper to taste

Directions

1. Season the chicken with garlic, rosemary, salt, and pepper.
2. Preheat the air fryer at 375 degrees F.
3. Place the grill pan accessory in the air fryer.
4. Grill for 35 minutes and make sure to flip the chicken every 10 minutes.

Nutrition

Calories:299; Carbs: 2.9g; Protein: 50.4g; Fat: 8.2g

Crab and Artichoke Dip

Preparation Time: 25 minutes

Servings: 4

Ingredients:

- 8 oz. cream cheese, soft
- 1 bunch green onions; minced
- 12 oz. jumbo crab meat
- 14 oz. canned artichoke hearts, drained and chopped.
- 1 ½ cups mozzarella; shredded
- 1 cup coconut cream
- 1 tbsp. lemon juice
- 1 tbsp. lemon juice
- A pinch of salt and black pepper

Directions:

1. In a bowl, combine all the ingredients except half of the cheese and whisk them really well.

2. Transfer this to a pan that fits your air fryer, introduce in the machine and cook at 400 °F for 15 minutes
3. Sprinkle the rest of the mozzarella on top and cook for 5 minutes more. Divide the mix into bowls and serve as a party dip

Nutrition:

Calories: 240; Fat: 8g; Fiber: 2g; Carbs: 4g; Protein: 14g

Simple & Delicious Spiced Apples

Preparation Time: 10 minutes

Cooking Time: 10 minutes

Servings: 4

Ingredients:

- 4 apples, sliced
- 1 tsp apple pie spice

- 2 tbsp ghee, melted
- 2 tbsp sugar

Directions:

1. Add apple slices into the mixing bowl.
2. Add remaining ingredients on top of apple slices and toss until well coated.
3. Transfer apple slices on instant vortex air fryer oven pan and air fry at 350 F for 10 minutes.
4. Top with ice cream and serve.

Nutrition:

Calories – 196 Protein – 0.6 g.Fat – 6.8 g.Carbs – 37.1 g.

Plum Cream

Preparation Time: 25 minutes

Servings: 4

Ingredients:

- 1 lb. plums, pitted and chopped.
- ¼ cup swerve
- 1 ½ cups heavy cream
- 1 tbsp. lemon juice

Directions:

1. Take a bowl and mix all the ingredients and whisk really well.
2. Divide this into 4 ramekins, put them in the air fryer and cook at 340°F for 20 minutes. Serve cold

Nutrition:

Calories: 171; Fat: 4g; Fiber: 2g; Carbs: 4g; Protein: 4g

Yogurt Cake

Preparation Time: 35 minutes

Servings: 12

Ingredients:

- 6 eggs, whisked
- 9 oz. coconut flour
- 8 oz. Greek yogurt
- 4 tbsp. stevia

- 1 tsp. baking powder
- 1 tsp. vanilla extract

Directions:

1. Take a bowl and mix all the ingredients and whisk well.
2. Pour this into a cake pan that fits the air fryer lined with parchment paper.
3. Put the pan in the air fryer and cook at 330 °F for 30 minutes

Nutrition:

Calories: 181; Fat: 13g; Fiber: 2g; Carbs: 4g; Protein: 5g

Dark Chocolate Cake

Preparation Time: 10 minutes

Cooking Time: 10 minutes

Servings: 4

Ingredients:

- 1½ tablespoons almond flour
- 2 eggs

- 3½ oz. unsalted butter
- 3½ oz. sugar free dark chocolate, chopped
- 3½ tablespoons swerve

Directions:

1. Preheat the Air fryer to 375 degrees F and grease 4 regular-sized ramekins.
2. Microwave all chocolate bits with butter in a bowl for about 3 minutes.
3. Remove from the microwave and whisk in the eggs and swerve.
4. Stir in the flour and mix well until smooth.
5. Transfer the mixture into the ramekins and arrange in the Air fryer basket.
6. Cook for about 10 minutes and dish out to serve.

Nutrition:

Calories: 379, Fat: 29.7g, Carbohydrates: 3.7g, Sugar: 1.3g, Protein: 5.2g, Sodium: 193mg

Ninja Pop-Tarts

Preparation Time: 10 minutes

Cooking Time: 1 hour; Serves 6

Ingredients:

Pop-tarts:

- 1 cup coconut flour
- ½ cup of ice-cold water
- 1 cup almond flour

Pop-tarts:

- ¼ teaspoon salt
- 2/3 cup very cold coconut oil
- 2 tablespoons swerve
- ½ teaspoon vanilla extract

Lemon Glaze:

- 1¼ cups powdered swerve
- 2 tablespoons lemon juice
- 1 teaspoon coconut oil, melted
- zest of 1 lemon
- ¼ teaspoon vanilla extract

Directions:

Pop-tarts:

1. Preheat the Air fryer to 375 degrees F and grease an Air fryer basket.
2. Mix all the flours, swerve, and salt in a bowl and stir in the coconut oil.
3. Mix well with a fork until an almond meal mixture is formed.
4. Stir in vanilla and 1 tablespoon of cold water and mix until a firm dough is formed.
5. Cut the dough into two equal pieces and spread in a thin sheet.
6. Cut each sheet into 12 equal-sized rectangles and transfer 4 rectangles in the Air fryer basket.
7. Cook for about 10 minutes and repeat with the remaining rectangles.

Lemon Glaze:

1. Meanwhile, mix all the ingredients for the lemon glaze and pour over the cooked tarts.
2. Top with sprinkles and serve.

Nutrition:

Calories: 368, Fat: 6g, Carbohydrates: 2.8g, Sugar: 2.9g, Protein: 7.2g, Sodium: 103mg

Coconut Donuts

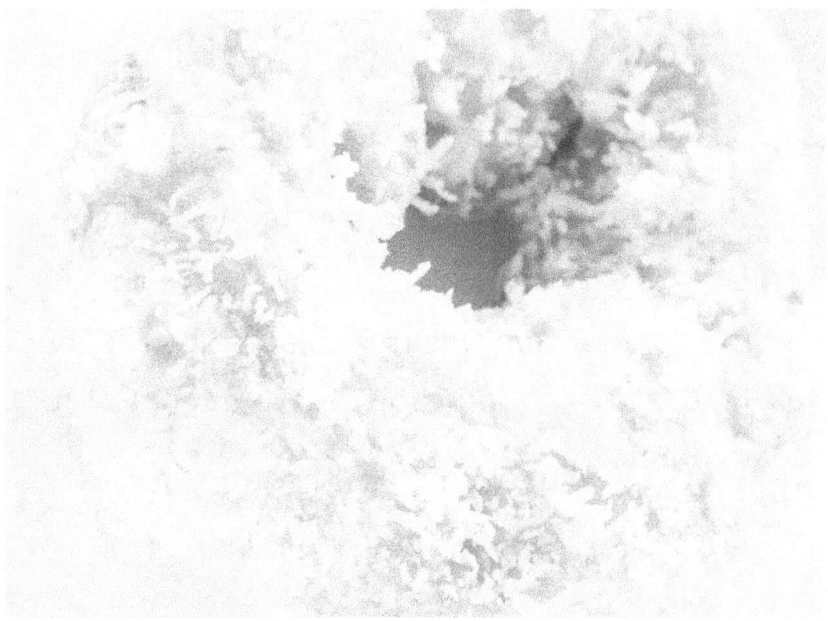

Preparation Time: 5 minutes

Cooking time: 15 minutes

Servings: 4

Ingredients:

- 8 ounces coconut flour
- 1 egg, whisked
- 2 tablespoons stevia

- 2 and ½ tablespoons butter, melted
- 1 teaspoon baking powder
- 4 ounces coconut milk

Directions:

1. In a bowl, mix all the ingredients: and whisk well.
2. Shape donuts from this mix, place them in your air fryer's basket and cook at 370 degrees F for 15 minutes.
3. Serve warm.

Nutrition:

Calories 190, fat 12, fiber 1, carbs 4, protein 6

Strawberry Jam

Preparation Time: 10 minutes

Cooking time: 20 minutes

Servings: 12

Ingredients:

- 8 ounces strawberries, sliced
- ¼ cup swerve
- 1 tablespoon lemon juice
- ¼ cup water

Directions:

1. In a pan that fits the air fryer, combine all the Ingredients:, put the pan in the machine and cook at 380 degrees F for 20 minutes.
2. Divide the mix into cups, cool down and serve.

Nutrition:

Calories 100, fat 1, fiber 0, carbs 1, protein 1

Amaretto Cream

Preparation Time: 18 minutes

Servings: 8

Ingredients:
- 12 oz. chocolate chips
- 1 cup heavy cream
- 1/2 cup butter; melted
- 1 cup sugar
- 2 tbsp. amaretto liqueur

Directions:
1. Place all of the ingredients in a bowl and stir
2. Pour the mixture into small ramekins and place in the air fryer
3. Cook at 320 °F for 12 minutes. Refrigerate / freeze for a while... best when served really cold.

Keto-Friendly Doughnut Recipe

Servings: 4

Cooking Time: 20 minutes

Ingredients

- ¼ cup coconut milk
- ¼ cup erythritol

- ¾ cup almond flour
- ¼ cup flaxseed meal
- 1 tablespoon cocoa powder
- 2 large eggs, beaten
- 1 teaspoon vanilla extract
- 3 tablespoons coconut oil

Directions:
1. Place all ingredients in a mixing bowl.
2. Mix until well-combined.
3. Scoop the dough into individual doughnut molds.
4. Preheat the air fryer for 5 minutes.
5. Cook for 20 minutes at 350 degree F.
6. Bake in batches if possible.

Nutrition:

Calories: 222; Carbohydrates: 5.1g; Protein: 3.9g; Fat: 20.7g

Pear Pastry Pouch

Servings: 4

Preparation Time: 15 minutes

Cooking Time: 15 minutes

Ingredients

- 2 small pears, peeled, cored and halved
- 4 puff pastry sheets
- 2 cups vanilla custard
- 2 tablespoons sugar
- 1 egg, lightly beaten
- Pinch of ground cinnamon
- 2 tablespoons whipped cream

Directions:

1. Carefully, make small cuts in each pear half.
2. Place a spoonful of vanilla custard and top with a pear half in the center of each pastry sheet.
3. In a bowl, mix together the sugar and cinnamon.

4. Sprinkle the sugar mixture evenly over pear halves.
5. Pinch the corners to shape into a pouch.
6. Now, coat each pear with egg.
7. Set the temperature of air fryer to 330 degrees F. Lightly, grease an air fryer basket.
8. Arrange pear pouches into the prepared air fryer basket in a single layer.
9. Air fry for about 15 minutes.
10. Remove from air fryer and transfer the pear pouches onto a platter.
11. Top with whipped cream and serve with the remaining custard.

Nutrition:

Calories: 467, Carbohydrate: 56.1g, Protein: 8g, Fat: 24.4g, Sugar: 36.5g, Sodium: 140mg

Chocolate Chip Pan Cookie

Preparation Time: 17 minutes

Servings: 4

Ingredients:

- 1 large egg.
- ½ cup blanched finely ground almond flour.
- ¼ cup powdered erythritol
- 2 tbsp. low-carb, sugar-free chocolate chips
- 2 tbsp. unsalted butter; softened.
- ½ tsp. unflavored gelatin
- ½ tsp. baking powder.
- ½ tsp. vanilla extract.

Directions:

1. Take a large bowl, mix almond flour and erythritol. Stir in butter, egg and gelatin until combined.
2. Stir in baking powder and vanilla and then fold in chocolate chips

3. Pour batter into 6-inch round baking pan. Place pan into the air fryer basket.
4. Adjust the temperature to 300 Degrees F and set the timer for 7 minutes
5. When fully cooked, the top will be golden brown and a toothpick inserted in center will come out clean. Let cool at least 10 minutes.

Nutrition:

Calories: 188; Protein: 5.6g; Fiber: 2.0g; Fat: 15.7g; Carbs: 16.8g

Notes

www.ingramcontent.com/pod-product-compliance
Lightning Source LLC
Chambersburg PA
CBHW070933080526
44589CB00013B/1494